Steve Parish

BRISBANE
Moments in a day

Brisbane Moments

Sunrise

Morning sparkles on the Brisbane River.

The river reflects the glittering high-rise buildings.

Warming Up

It's too nice a morning to stay indoors.

As the day warms up, so does the city.

Hidden amongst the city's hustle and bustle, there are
special places to savour the morning.

Noon

Splendid architecture recalls Brisbane's
beginnings and achievements.

In a river city, beautiful bridges are a must.

On the move: the city's lunchtime rush.

Public art brightens the city.

Enjoying the afternoon sun at South Bank.

Sun and sand in the city.

Brisbane culture: remembering and celebrating.

Fine food, good company and good shopping
make for a pleasant afternoon.

All over the city, café precincts and pubs offer an inviting
way to while away the afternoon.

There are many gardens in which to take in the
colour and sunshine, or just relax in the shade.

Timber and tin: Brisbane houses are designed
to catch the afternoon breezes.

Winding Down

The western sun lights up Kangaroo Point.

Time to head home - or on to the evening's fun.

Fans are loyal to their teams, whatever the code.

Sunset

The fading light casts a warm glow over the city.

The warm weather is perfect for dining al fresco.

above Fortitude Valley and Chinatown come to life at night.

right The sky is ablaze during River*fire*.

Arts, culture and fine dining are provided at South Bank.

Index

Note: For multiple-image pages, locations are listed in a clockwise direction from top left.